leapfrog
Learners

Football

by Annabelle Lynch

First published in 2013 by
Franklin Watts
338 Euston Road
London
NW1 3BH

Franklin Watts Australia
Level 17/207 Kent Street
Sydney, NSW 2000

Picture credits: Chris Brunskill/AMA/Matthew Ashton/
AMA/Corbis: 14-15. Maxisport/Shutterstock: 7. moodboard/
Corbis: 9. Natursports/Shutterstock: cover, 13.
Ron Nickel/Design Pics/Corbis: 5. Kiyoshi Ota/Getty
Images: 17. kristian sekulic/istockphoto: 21.
Laszio Szirtesi/Shutterstock: 11. Daniel
Dal Zennaro/epa/Corbis: title page, 18.

A CIP catalogue record for this book is
available from the British Library.

Dewey number: 796.3

ISBN 978 1 4451 1641 9 (hbk)
ISBN 978 1 4451 1647 1 (pbk)

Series Editor: Julia Bird
Picture Researcher: Diana Morris
Series Advisor: Catherine Glavina
Series Designer: Peter Scoulding

Franklin Watts is a division of Hachette Children's Books,
an Hachette UK company. www.hachette.co.uk

Contents

The words in **bold** can be found in the glossary.

Football is fun!

Football is the world's favourite game. People play it everywhere.

All you need to play football is a ball.

Stadiums

Some football matches are played in **stadiums**. Thousands of people come to watch big matches.

Have you ever been to a football match?

In attack

A football team
has 11 players.
Forwards try
to score goals
for the team.

GOAL!

For the defence

The **defenders** and goalkeeper work together. They stop players from the other team scoring goals.

The goalkeeper can use his hands to stop the ball going into the goal.

Famous player

Lionel Messi is one of the best football players in the world. He uses skill and tricks to beat defenders.

Messi comes from a country called Argentina.

Great team

Spain is the best football team in the world today.

Spain play in a red and yellow kit.

They have won three **international** football **competitions** in a row!

The fans

Football fans bring a match to life. Fans shout, sing songs and wave scarves and flags to **support** their team.

Every football team has its own scarf.

World Cups

World Cup competitions bring fans and football teams together. Everyone wants their country to win!

Italy have won the World Cup four times.

Join in!

Playing football is fun, and it is good for you too. Why not grab some friends and a ball and play today?

You can play football in the playground, in the park or even in your own garden.

Competitions - when teams play against each other to find out who is the best

Defenders - players who try to stop the other team scoring goals

Forwards - players who try to score goals

International - from different countries

Stadium - big buildings where people go to watch sport and other events

Support - to cheer on

Websites:

http://www.footee.com

http://www.premierleague.com/en-gb/kids.html

Every effort has been made by the Publishers to ensure that the websites are suitable for children, and that they contain no inappropriate or offensive material. However, because of the nature of the Internet, it is impossible to guarantee that the contents of these sites will not be altered. We strongly advise that Internet access is supervised by a responsible adult.

Quiz

Use the information in the book to answer these questions.

1. What is the name for a big building where football matches are played?

2. How many players does a football team have?

3. Which players work together to stop the other team scoring goals?

4. Which country does Lionel Messi come from?

5. How do football fans support their team?

(The answers are on page 24.)

Answers

1. A stadium
2. Eleven
3. Defenders and the goalkeeper
4. Argentina
5. They shout, sing songs and wave scarves and flags.

Index